The Work-at-Home Entrepreneur's Guide to Success

By Deborah L. Killion, Entrepreneur

I0468571

TABLE OF CONTENTS

INTRODUCTION

This book is about my journey from a full-time employee to almost full-time work-at-home entrepreneur. I have worked as a teacher, counselor, call center agent, radio announcer, fast food employee, Avon salesperson, and countless other jobs before discovering my true calling. I now work as a work-at-home entrepreneur with my technology and media production business, and writing career. I write for *Fortune 500* companies and others, writing high level content to increase traffic and sales to their websites and businesses. I plan to launch a virtual global online company in early 2015 which will feature a fully stocked media store, and offer my production and writing services to Fortune 500 and celebrity clients.

This book is for you, my fellow work-at-home entrepreneur, or for the person who wants to be a work-at-home entrepreneur. The key is to make it like an employment position, by following a pattern of behaviors and strategies to make sure you are bringing in the money. Read on to find out how I made it work for me! Happy sailing!

Words: 8,654

I. INDEPENDENT CONTRACTOR OR EMPLOYEE: THAT IS THE QUESTION

Before you decide what niche area to get into or the other details in launching your work-at-home career, the first thing you should consider is whether you want to be an *employee* or an *independent contractor*. Both statuses have their advantages and both you can work from your home environment.

Here is some information on both, and the differences, so that you can make a more informed decision on which is right for you:

Employee- The main difference is that, as an employee, you normally will work for only one company and your employment is usually based on a specific contract of employment. The perks are that you may be offered a benefits package, vacation time, contributions to 401K plans, dental and medical insurance, and more. One company I interviewed with offered an $80,000 per year salary, unlimited sick days, 100% coverage on medical insurance, and a free computer! While these opportunities may be rare, they are out there. I will show you some place to find jobs like this at the end of my eBook. But please read it all the way through, as I also put some links and other valuable resources throughout the book as well. In the meantime, here is one place to start. They offer very good job opportunities on both a part-time and full-time level which you can apply to. It does cost $14.95 per month to be a premium member, but it's worth it. I have gotten several writing jobs this way and continue to do so!

Try this: http://www.flexjobs.com. And let me know if you have success! By the way, you can find both "employee" and "contractor" jobs here, but most are "contractor" jobs.

Contractor- As opposed to employee status, if you work as an independent contractor, you are your own boss. You work your own hours, decide when or how much to work, and take on whichever jobs you prefer. Companies are outsourcing more and more independent contractor jobs nowadays. It is a very good strategy for a big company. Think about it. If you're a big company, and the economy is in bad shape, and you need the most efficient ROI (return on your investment), which would you rather have? A full-time employee who works 40 hours per week, and pay them for every hour, or an independent contractor, whom you only pay for the time worked?

Not to mention that many of those hours may be spent by that employee having coffee, talking to other co-workers about non-work issues, making personal calls, and checking their Face Book accounts. This is why more companies are choosing to hire outside work for specific tasks. When they do this, they also tend to get more specialists who focus on one thing and bring a fresh perspective to their company. It's a no-brainer.

WHAT DOES THIS MEAN FOR YOU?

So, as an independent contractor, this means you can work for several companies at a time, or just one, doing the things you do best. You can set your own hours, schedule family events and other responsibilities around your work load, and pick and choose how much time you wish to spend on different jobs. Likewise, if you take on too much, you can pull back a bit from some of the jobs and focus on the ones that pay the most, setting aside those which aren't worth your time.

THE DOWN SIDE

The down side to independent contracting is that you have no one to answer to except yourself (though that is also the positive side). You have to file your own taxes, keep accurate records yourself, get your own medical insurance, and contribute to your own 401K plans. In other words, you're on your own! You, and only you determine your own income, and you have only yourself to blame if you don't succeed. You are the captain of your own ship! And if she runs aground, you can't blame it on an iceberg!

THE BOTTOM LINE

Admittedly, I like being my own boss! Though there are times I wish I had someone to do all of that for me. And I have worked through days as a freelance writer and media producer, where I forgot to eat lunch! I got so busy I just kept on working! And with no "boss" to tell me to go eat, I didn't even notice!

But, the bottom line is, as one of my famous entrepreneur friends said once, "Ask yourself if you really want to do this? Do you want to do it or not?" (Tom Smiley, from his audio book, "Starting Your Home Business.") And Tom is right. You have to decide at this moment if you are an "entrepreneur" or as Mark Cuban (another person I've chatted with) from the famous "Shark Tank" show which now airs on ABC, called people who wanted to be an entrepreneur but didn't have what it took. He referred to these wannabes as "a 'wantrepreneur.'" In other words, do you have what it takes to really make it work? Or are you just dreaming? Read on to find out!

II.TAKING THE PLUNGE TO FULL-TIME ENTREPRENEUR

The most difficult step to take when becoming a full-time entrepreneur is making the adjustment from "part-time," which usually involved working as an employee too for someone else during the day, to full-time "work-at-home guru," which means you work only for yourself.

Some of the challenges you will face involve adjusting to the "at home" environment, scheduling time to spend with family and other responsibilities, and making sure you stay productive (time management). We will discuss some of these later in the book. First, let's talk about the main reason this transition is hard to do for some: MONEY.

Let's face it. Working for someone else is easy. They pay you at a regular time each month, take insurance out automatically, tell you when to work and when to go home, and basically own your life. Oh yeah, that's one of the reasons you wanted to be an entrepreneur in the first place: the freedom from a boss who runs your life and is in control of your time. But, when you break away from this, though the freedom is definitely worth it, you will now have to make your own money 100% of the time. Once you walk out of a job, you may not be able to come back, especially if your reason for leaving was "to run your own business."

So, before you give the boss your resignation letter, make sure you have the following things in place:

a. Find a niche that people want and need. I will discuss this in chapter 4 in much more detail, but think about how you are going to fill a need in your local area, or even a larger area. If you do not find an area that people will pay for, you cannot make any money.
b. Follow the money. This is discussed in chapter 8, but think now about the way you are going to make money. This process involves everything from how

much to charge, how to market your talents, whether to hire helpers, and more.

c. Set up a separate business account. You need a business bank account that is separate and apart from your personal accounts. This is very important, especially around tax time, so you can keep your personal expenditures and income separate from the business. If you have separate accounts for business, you can just ask for a statement or print these out monthly to keep up with the income and outgo of the business.

d. Create a schedule. Before you take the plunge to full-time entrepreneurship, make sure you have created a schedule for yourself. Understand that this can change, and you can remain flexible. But having a general schedule or a set of goals on projects will keep you focused. And this is absolutely imperative if you are going to be successful as a work-at-home entrepreneur.

e. Talk to other entrepreneurs. Much of what I have learned to make my business successful has been due to the intermingling and networking with other successful business owners. Find out what they did to become successful and emulate their techniques within your own business when you can.

Once you are ready, decide you will make it work no matter what! More has been accomplished with a determined attitude than with any other single factor. So, as Tom Smiley said, decide if you are going to do this or not, then give it all you've got. In chapter 3, we will discuss how to fire your boss and never look back!

III. HOW TO "FIRE YOUR BOSS" AND NEVER LOOK BACK

The most important thing you must do in order to "fire your boss" is to be absolutely determined that you are going to make it work. Secondly, you must KNOW without any doubt that you have the resources to get started, (See chapter 15), and you must be secure in the notion that you can create your own income from here on. Do not go to your boss with the idea that you are working on a way to quit. (I don't think you would do this anyway!) But don't talk too much to co-workers about your new found independence, until you are ready to do it! Or you may be doing it earlier than you thought!

The old cliché, "Loose lips sink ships," comes to mind here. To take the cliché even more annoyingly further: You do not want to abandon the ship, until you are sure your own ship is waiting in the wings and ready to board!

Have a business plan! Don't even think about starting a business, any business, without a business plan. Even if you have to change it a thousand times a week, a working business plan of what your goals are, and a clear, succinct step-by-step procedure to get there is absolutely critical for success. Admittedly, I am still figuring mine out, but I do have a working business plan, which I look at and revisit at least one per month, to see if I'm on target. If I leave you with nothing else than this, put 'having a business plan' on the top of your list when starting a business.

This works seamlessly with goal-setting too and we discuss this in chapter 12. Read on.

IV.DECIDING ON A NICHE MARKET

As mentioned earlier, you must decide on a niche area, or a specialty area that is marketable. There are many opinions on how to do this. One way is to look around your own neighborhood and see what the need is. Does your neighborhood have an "errand service?" Do they need one? If you are willing to do what it takes, you could be the "go-to" person for local errands.

Communities with a high population of older citizens or disabled persons who cannot do things for themselves would be a good market for this service. How about a dog walking service? It is estimated that over half the population of the world has a dog or other pet. Now narrow it down. How many of those who have pets need someone to walk their dog and don't have time to do it themselves? Put an ad in the local paper and see what results you get. This is actually another way to decide on a niche. I have never tried this myself, except with different services I already offer, but here's an idea you could try: Put different ads in the paper the same week offering different services and see who bites! See which niche generated the most interest and focus on that one. Of course, make sure you can deliver though, if they call about one of the other ads, so put in things you can really do! ☺

The best way to decide on a niche is to think about what you like, what you do well, and where the market is. Let's face it, you could have a great idea, or a thousand great ideas, but without a market, it's dead in the water. Think about where your market is, or target audience for your product(s) or service. Then focus on them. In all of your ads, talk to that audience specifically. That should produce the results you need.

STRATEGIES TO THINK ABOUT WHEN CHOOSING A NICHE

One theory is that you should go after what everyone wants. The people who believe in this argument say this because they believe that you shouldn't try to invent a new niche that few are in. This is one of the hardest tasks to do, and involves immense global marketing efforts to generate interest in the new area. It has been done though. But most experts agree you should get into a field others are already in. This way the market has already been tested and you know what you have will sell. While it could be argued this is harder due to the competition, at least you know you have a product or service that people want, and you know where the market is.

V. START-UP COSTS

So, now let's be pragmatic. I know this is the "dream killer" for many, but it shouldn't be. You've always heard there are 'dreamers' and 'doers,' but the only dreamers who realize their dreams are the ones who took specific actions to make their dream happen. So decide which you are. Fortunately, for myself, I am both. I am a big, ambitious dreamer "artsy fartsy," who is just daring enough to think I can change the world with my gift of creative glee. I'm one of the " crazy ones" Steve Jobs talked about in his ad he created before he died, talking to future entrepreneurs. But, at the same time, I dare to get out my bed every morning and do what it takes, step-by-step! And you can too!

One very common quality in all successful entrepreneurs is their undying motivation to succeed, no matter what. If you have that fire, you'll make it happen.

Now, regarding start-up costs....

Another very important factor to consider before launching out on your own, especially if you go full-time with this, is the start-up cost of running your own business. So important is this that may entrepreneurs say you should not even consider starting any business until you have a great deal of money behind you, saved up, or stocked away. That being said, I will tell you that I started my company with practically zero investment dollars from myself or anyone else, and rented a small space downtown in my town of 6500 people. I've always had a saying I have lived by, "Just do something, anything, and keep moving forward. That way you are moving toward something." And this has always worked for me.

My business is digital media production and creation for businesses, and content writing, and I already had most of my equipment I needed to get started. So the only overhead and start-up costs I really had was renting the space for $400 per month, the utilities for the business, and supplies, etc. But I quickly realized that what I was doing wasn't working for my business, so after a year of frustrations, I moved out and moved back home.

There, my overhead was next to nothing, and I could focus on my goals with no distractions. And I am doing very well! There's nothing wrong with running your business from your home. Some of the most successful entrepreneurs I know did the same. Ever heard of Steve Jobs? Bill Gates? Daymond John, owner of FUBU, the internationally famous clothing line and co-star of "Shark Tank?" These are just a few examples of people who successfully ran their businesses from their homes, until they became too large to do so. But even very large corporations are still being started and maintained from people's basements, garages, and homes today. So the work-at-home model does work, even for big business!

VI. FINDING A NEED

We talked earlier about finding a need and developing your business in a niche area. This is very important. You want to focus on finding something people will want and something they are willing to pay for. On the most basic level, this has to do with finding something people need, rather than just something people "want." So think about a need you think your own area has, and then expand that to consider whether the whole world might need it. We are working toward "global thinking" here because remember, as a "work-at-home entrepreneur," your goal is to establish a company that has the potential to be very big. I think in "global" terms because I am in the process of launching a global company in 2015. Everything I do is leading me toward that goal. But, if you are not quite this ambitious, look instead for something that will satisfy a need in your own area, town, or state and move on from there.

ONE PERSONAL NOTE

I have a friend who I offered to promote on my global website and told her about a service which would get her business noticed on a global level. She is a professional photographer and takes beautiful creative pictures for weddings and all kinds of other special events. But she said that she wanted to keep the business regional. And that is her choice and that's okay. You certainly do not want to launch a global business if you do not want to service this large of a market. Because, like Pandora's Box, once you open this treasure trove, and unleash your business on the world, it is very difficult to scale it down again to a smaller, manageable level again. So decide right off how big you want to make this thing, and base your decisions and strategies on that.

VII. DO WHAT YOU LOVE

There was a book published on hard copy years ago entitled, *Do What You Love, the Money will Follow.(by Marsha Sinetar)(1989)* I noticed the eBook to this work is available on Amazon Kindle. Get it here: http://www.amazon.com/What-Love-Money-Follow-ebook/dp/0440501601. It is a great book on how to find what you do best in life and make money from it.

I agree with the author on this point. It is vitally important to love what you do and do what you love. It is also true that, the more you love something, the more you will do it, and the better you will get at it. So while I believe that it is not enough alone to do what you love, if you are doing something you hate, I can pretty much guarantee you will fail. Remember, you are not working for someone else when you are a work-at-home (or any other kind) of entrepreneur. You are working for yourself. This means you are generating your own income night and day. You have only yourself to answer to, so you must be the worst kind of boss. You must be even worse than that boss you ran away from to do this entrepreneur thing in the first place!

MY FACEBOOK POST

I once posted on Face book that "I quit my day job to get away from the worst boss in the world, so that I could make my money on my own, decide my own schedule, and experience financial freedom. What I didn't realize was that, in order to achieve that, I had to BE the worst boss in the world to myself to accomplish that!" How ironic! But true! If I do not discipline myself to sit down and work and crank out another article, or work on another eBook, then I do not get paid! It's as simple as that. Perhaps the Bible verse that says, 'If a man not work, then neither shall he eat," was written solely for the work-at-home entrepreneur!

That being said, you do still have the freedom to schedule your work whenever you see fit, and focus on your own goals and projects, rather than the goals and projects of someone else. That is why it is so appealing to become a work-at-home guru rather than toil away at the desk of another company. It is also an argument for being an independent contractor, rather than an employee, whether you work inside or outside your home environment.

It all comes down to this: You're either going to feed the goals and dreams of another company or your own goals and dreams. <u>What will your choice be?</u>
Another saying that may help you to see this in the proper perspective is:

"You've either got to figure it out, or go work for someone else who has figured it out." -(Deborah L Killion, Entrepreneur)

So find something you love and go do it with all your might. But don't do it just yet. In the next chapter, I will talk about how to follow the money, because that is, after all, "the bottom line."

VIII. FOLLOW THE MONEY

My favorite entrepreneur, Mark Cuban, has often said this on the ABC "Shark Tank" program to the hopeful entrepreneurs who present their business to the shark panel on the show. And he's right. I have applied his ideas in my own business and I have created more income for myself just by living this credo.

But, how do you know which opportunities will make you the most money or ROI (return on your investment?) Some of this, admittedly, is a trial-and-error process, but you can also study how others have done in a similar area, and try to emulate their success by applying some of the same principles.

In a nutshell, "following the money" means to spend the majority of your time on the things which provide you with a maximum ROI (return on investment) of your time and money. And spend less time on those things that do not. For example, related to my own business of freelance writing and media content production, I used to have a service called "digital scrap booking." Actually, I still offer it. But it's never in my advertising. Any guesses why not? Right! It didn't sell! At least not locally. So why spend advertising dollars and print beautiful ads and promote something that is not selling? Instead, I choose now to focus on the most popular services we offer, such as VHS-to-DVD conversions, DVD mass duplications, digital video production, file conversions, etc. These sell well, even in my own small town, so I hit these harder in both the advertising and the time I spend to help the business grow.

Lesson: Weed out the things that don't work and follow the money. Watch the trends but stick close to your niche market and follow the money! You're so right, Mark!

A WORD ABOUT MOBILE MEDIA

A chapter on following the money would not be complete without mentioning mobile media. Mobile media (the hardware and the mobile apps, etc.) has increased in sales beyond anyone's imagination the past few years and months and it is estimated that it will continue to grow exponentially for the foreseeable future. Big business is cutting their advertising budget of their more traditional national television ads in favor of You Tube and online marketing and advertising. Why? <u>They are going where the people are</u>! That is the same reason radio and TV stations are getting online too! Over 500 million people per month are said to frequent You Tube searches each month to see what they can see. And that's too big a part of the market to ignore. As I said in an article for a Fortune 500 client awhile back, "500 million people can't be wrong!" By the way, I had 5 bids on that article, so they must agree with me! So another way of following the money is to go where the people are. And they are all on mobile media, shopping, making appointments, and on social media like Face Book talking to their friends.

IX. ARE YOU OBSESSED?

One of my favorite sayings is one I made up myself: "The difference between excellence and genius is obsession." At least, I think I made it up. I've never head it quite put that way, so if anyone else has ever thought that up, we can share in the glory. The point is, for those of us who make our own money with our own efforts, it is almost crucial that we become obsessed with our work and our specialty. For example, I am a video producer. I produce high-quality digital (HD) video. I have a degree in Radio-TV and that's puts me above many in terms of credibility. I work hard on client projects and try to do what they like. They pay me for this service. They usually like it. But am I obsessed? Steven Spielberg is obsessed. I have read his entire story about how he broke into the business of filmmaking and made a name for himself, how he rode in on a tourist trolley and set up an office in the back lot of Universal Studios, how he snuck around and got Goldie Hawn to star in a $10,000 film and then showed it to studio executives…how he slowly but surely worked his way up the ranks by showing off his talent as a superb filmmaker, waiting till the time was right to expose his art to the powers that be in Hollywood.

And now, as CEO of one of the biggest motion picture companies in the world, he carries that same obsession with him, that same dedication to brilliance and utter perfection in his art, to every single film he creates. Now that's obsession folks! Do you have it? Do you have that burning desire to be the best of the best? I'm not sure I have it for filmmaking alone. I love video production and filmmaking but I've realize lately my true passion is in the writing and media creation process. So I have spent the past 6 months honing in on my talents in this, writing for multiple publishers, contacting Fortune 500 companies, talking to the 'sharks' like Mark Cuban, Kevin O'Leary, and entrepreneur, Donald Trump on Twitter, and adding Hollywood celebrities to my Face Book and Twitter accounts. Some of them have even added me back! I have made the connections necessary to take my business to a higher level. But, more importantly, I have worked every day to find ways to make my business work! And at the end of this year, I will be working this 100% full-time and I am determined to make it work. So, yes, I think now I can officially say I am obsessed…obsessed with success. And for the first time, it is starting to pay off for me.

So do I believe that obsession is the key to success? YES, YES, and YES!!!

X. SETTING BOUNDARIES

This chapter talks about the importance of setting boundaries for working moms and parents, but it also has to do with your lifestyle as a "work-at-home" expert, with the goal being to maximize your time. You also need to make sure your work area stays a "work area," and is not open to the whole family or others, especially during work hours. If you have small children, this can be a problem. I used to work in a call center job and I had nothing but an occasional screeching sound coming from my cockatiel who wanted attention, or the postman leaving a package I needed to sign for. I can't imagine the challenges of the single mom trying to juggle a crying two-year-old with calls and clients at the same time, while keeping their environment "free of interruptions!" This is certainly a challenge I am sure for those unlike me with families and other in your home.

This is why, if you truly want to make this work, and you do happen to be a single mom or other staying home with children, you have to plan for this too. Plan to hire a babysitter to stay with your children at specific times that are the busiest for your work-at-home business. Consider taking children to a nearby daycare or the babysitter's home instead, so that you could pick them up for awhile during one of your breaks.

It is understandable that there are many moms out there probably reading my book who would like easy answers to this problem. But, the truth is, there aren't any. If you really want to do this, you have to clear the obstacles. So plan for the kids to be elsewhere while you're working or you will not be able to focus. Another suggestion might be, if you have exceptionally quiet, well-behaved children, you could perhaps write down what their food and sleep schedule is and plan your working hours when they are sleeping, etc. However, this will get to be tricky over time and there will be times you'll find yourself having to choose between the child's needs, and the needs of your customers.

On a humorous note, I heard of a lady in a nearby town who nursed her kids "on the job," between clients. This is the extreme of trying to be a "super mom" and it often caused embarrassing situations for both her and her patients. But I guess it also proves that, where there's a will, there's a way. So think about your children's habits and behaviors before you embark on any career as a work-at-home mom or entrepreneur.

Remember, when you're in business for yourself, your business is your baby, and it must come first most of the time, if you are going to make it work.

But, in defense of "stay at home mom's," having kids at home is not the only way you can be distracted or be a poor manager of your time. I'm single but if I get up at 11am, watch TV for an hour, goof off and just generally dawdle, it produces the same non-productive effect as it would if I had 3 kids. Manage your time, no matter what your situation! This is a necessary requirement for success as a work-at-home entrepreneur.

XI. SOMEWHERE OVER THE RAINBOW

Dorothy in "The Wizard of Oz" sang this song, "Somewhere over the Rainbow," as an illustration of someone dreaming of a place that is wonderful, filled with joy and friendship, riches, and all that one could need. It brings to mind all of the things that we remember from our childhood and all of the things that we love and desire the world to be.

But the truth is, this is just wishful thinking. There is no "pot of gold," at the end of that rainbow. There is no "Sanctuary," no "Get Rich Quick" plan or scheme. As Kevin Costner said in the famous movie, "Thirteen Days," about the Cuban missile crisis, "there is no wise old man, there is no quick fix…hell, there's just _us_."

And he's right. Unlike an employee relationship where you could go to a boss or supervisor and ask for help, you are on your own as an entrepreneur. That is why you got in this game to begin with. You may have resources you can turn to, and friends who might give you advice. But, I've heard it said by another of my famous entrepreneur friends, "Never take advice from someone who has less to lose than you from the result." (My friends in the "Shark Tank" said that too.) As an entrepreneur, you become your own best friend, and you have only yourself as a worst enemy if it fails. So do the best you can do to secure your interests, and click your heels three times. You are a work-at-home entrepreneur and there's no place like home!!

XII. REACHING YOUR GOALS

There have been many books written on setting and reaching your goals. Books such as Stephen Covey's 7 Habits of Highly Effective People (https://www.stephencovey.com/7habits/7habits.php) talks about the characteristics prevalent in effective people who know how to set goals and reach them and how to quit blaming your upbringing or your environment or the past for your failures. In their book, Goal Setting: How to Create an Action Plan and Achieve Your Goals, (http://www.amazon.com/Goal-Setting-Create-Achieve-Worksmart/dp/0814401694/ref=sr_1_8?s=books&ie=UTF8&qid=1380588217&sr=1-8&keywords=goal+setting), Susan B. Wilson and Michael S. Dobson explain how to set realistic goals and reach them over time, and in a systematic manner. But the most important element of goal setting is to make the goals obtainable, to write down a time table in which to achieve them, and fit them into your business plan. Here are a few important points to keep in mind when setting goals for your business or yourself:

Make them attainable but challenging. If you make the goal too easy, it will not require enough work on your part to keep you reaching higher. If they are too hard, you will feel like giving up too easily. Apply psychology to yourself by allowing yourself to grow into the goal gradually, stretching yourself just enough to keep moving forward. For example, if you are selling online for eBay, and you made $500 last month, it is not a realistic goal to assume you could make $5000 the next month. Instead, step up to the next level and put the goal at $750 per month, and gradually work from that upwards. Your goal may eventually be to reach $5000 per month, but the reality is that it takes time to build a clientele, repeat customers, and deal with wholesalers in such a way to bring it up to this level. So, while that is a worthy goal, start small and move up and you will be more likely to stick with it.

Make the goal worthwhile to your business. Always have in the back of your mind what is best for your business. Even if you want to add a local department store to your business, if it is not best for the business, don't do it. Add only things that can add potential value for your business in the long run, and drop the rest.

Bite off little pieces. I've already overdone clichés in this eBook, but I have to mention one more: Rome was not built in a day. Your business won't be either. There are no "get rich quick" plans, at least no legitimate ones. It's all about hard work, and a gradual grinding away at small tasks which lead to the acquisition of larger goals. So have several small goals you wish to accomplish, such as "outsource ad campaign to local contractors," "write up a white paper for business," or "design a business website." Even these smaller tasks can take a long time from start to completion, but the key is to get started on some of the small but important steps to lead your business to success.

<u>Monitor and adjust weekly.</u> Just like you must do in life, check the progress of your goals regularly, to see how you are doing. This can include anything from sophisticated online analytical tools to simply picking up the phone and checking for customer satisfaction. Every little thing you do may seem a small thing in and of itself, but it can mean something bigger down the road to the overall success of your business.

<u>Set new goals after reaching current ones.</u> As a business owner, you always want to keep growing, adding new things, trying new approaches, and monitoring the results. This can be done through a variety of means, but as soon as you reach one goal, whether it is a financial goal or otherwise, set a new, higher one to reach for. The more you challenge yourself to reach new levels, the quicker you will see the results you are trying to achieve.

HOW I SET GOALS

I spoke earlier about setting schedules. What I do is actually more "task oriented," rather than "hour oriented." I find that it just works better for me. For example, as a freelance writer for Fortune 500 companies, I may set a goal of 25 articles for the week to put in on a content writing site I write for. This is because I know that if I write 25 articles, I will probably sell about half of these within a week or so, and that produces about $300-$500 worth of income just on that one goal. This is just a part of my income I receive from my freelance writing part of my business, not counting all the other things I do within my media production, app creation, audio book production, etc. part of the business. But the issue is I stay focused on the money and the "product" I am putting out, more than the time I spend.

THE IMPORTANCE OF "TIME"

That being said, time is my most valuable commodity. (I think Mark Cuban said that too!) So I guard it religiously. I try to make sure I am not wasting time during the day and check myself; to be sure I am staying focused on the goal.

(However, it is okay to engage in a few small mental breaks, such as playing my hamburger game on my mobile tablet or phone! LOL! I love the childish games the best!) Just make sure you are disciplined enough to get right back to work on the things that are making you money the most. But save some time to do what you want also, and on weekends when you can.

I love setting my own schedule and focusing on my goals. I even find the time to do some "pro bono" (free work) for my local church. My preacher and I have even become good friends! So, focus on your work, but also save some time for family and friends, and to be with those you enjoy being with too. This gives more balance to your life.

IN A NUTSHELL

In a nutshell, goal-setting is a personal thing. It will not be the same for everyone, or for every business. Just make sure that you are continually setting new, higher goals to achieve once you have reached the first one, and monitor your progress along the way. Also, do not compare yourself to others. While I am very ambitious and competitive, I never try to compete with others, only myself. If I am achieving higher than I did the week before, the day before, the year before, I consider myself on the road to success.

It's fine if I show everyone up with my freelance writing excellence or other skills, (and I often have "wowed" publishers and sold multiple articles in a day, while others fell by the wayside), but I still mainly compare myself to myself. That keeps me moving forward without feeling I'm in a contest with others around me or in the same industry.

"Setting a goal is not the main thing. It is deciding how you will go about achieving it and staying with that plan". ~ Tom Landry ~

XIII. SOME FINAL POINTERS

As I prepare to close this first eBook, I will leave you with some sound advice. Don't try to do too much too soon. Don't overextend yourself. Don't overspend. Don't hire people at first. Don't place too many ads. Don't get into debt!! Think big, but realize you have to start small. I have been in business for myself around 5 years now and was a "serial entrepreneur." I tried every type of work-at-home opportunity you could possibly think of, until I finally found what I should be doing-focusing on my own online business in the field of content writing and media creation. I have worked at online call centers, insurance sales, video transcription, Mary Kay, Avon, eLance, and just about every other opportunity there is out there. Luckily, because I was careful and researched the opportunities, I never got scammed. But they did not all produce the level of income I wanted. So that's why I moved on and started focusing on my own business.

I will share my experiences with you in a future eBook about the above opportunities. I realize not everyone wants to be the next Mark Cuban or Donald Trump like I do and set the world on fire. Some people reading this eBook may just want to find a legitimate work-at-home opportunity that fits their needs and make a little money on the side. Or perhaps you just want to find a full-time work@home opportunity and focus primarily on that. That's fine too! If that is the case, then please look for the launch of my next eBook, which will actually be a series of shorter eBooks on particular work-at-home opportunities like these mentioned above.

I have become such an expert at work@home jobs that Terry Bradshaw actually used some of my material in one of his episodes of "Net Worth TV," on national television, as well as his financial blog. And one of my publishers in Florida interviewed me for You Tube about work@home opportunities as well. You can check out some of these at: http://stretcher.com. Gary Foreman is one of my publishers and he has been quoted by USA TODAY, Wall Street

Journal, and other financial publications in the past. He has his own online publication now in Bradenton Beach, Florida which deals with financial issues and consumer money tips.

My final pointer is to believe in yourself. If you do not believe you will be successful, how can anyone else believe in you? You have to sell yourself first. So take an assertiveness training class if necessary, but get up each day telling yourself you are going to have the best day ever in moving closer to your goals. Step-by-step, you'll do it!

XIV. RESOURCES FOR FURTHER RESEARCH

Because I know how having a plethora of links to great opportunities has helped me in the past in my quest for work-at-home jobs, I have compiled a list of what I believe to be some of the best links on the web for finding legitimate work-at-home opportunities. In addition, I am collecting the emails of anyone out there who would like to be on my newsletter list of the best work at home opportunities should I come across new information that will help you. I do a lot of research on this and would love to help you in your job search. If you want to be on a future email list to receive updates on new work-at-home opportunities or other information I come across, go to my main website at: http://smalltownglobal.com and put "SUBSCRIBE" in the subject. When I get a collection of subscribers, I will send you regular information as I come across it, to help you further in your quest for entrepreneurial independence. The site officially launches around Jan. 2015 but you can check out the main page now and email us with the online contact form.

Check out our corporate website, still in the beginning phases here:

http://smalltownglobal.com.

Well, enough talk. That should get you started.

Here are the links:

AVOIDING SCAMS

http://www.consumer.ftc.gov/articles/0175-work-home-businesses

http://www.usatoday.com/story/money/personalfinance/2012/12/30/money-quick-tips-work-at-home-options/1770859/

http://usatoday30.usatoday.com/money/smallbusiness/2010-06-29-workathome29_VA_N.htm

JOB LINKS (INDEPENDENT CONTRACTOR POSITIONS)

CALL CENTER/CUSTOMER SERVICE JOBS

http://join.liveops.com
http://partner.arise.com/
http://www.contractworld.jobs/

DATABASE OF WORK@HOME JOBS

http://www.wahm.com/

FOR TEACHERS AND TUTORS
http://k12.com
http://educate-online.com
http://tutor.com
http://eduboard.com (BRAND NEW!)
http://recruit.tutorabc.com/program/applynow.asp (BRAND NEW!)

MICRO JOBS (DATA PROCESSING, ETC.)

http://mturk.com (an Amazon company-micro jobs)
https://www.mobileworks.com/

COSMETIC INDUSTRY
http://marykay.com
http://avon.com

JOB BOARDS
http://elance.com
http://odesk.com
http://freelancer.com

START-UP BUSINESS OPPORTUNITIES

http://www.workwithamyjacobs.com/

http://www.mydoterra.com/182805/

http://www.nomorewicks.com/candle_business

http://www.tinagowans.labellabaskets.com/

http://www.fashionablyou.com/ (NEW!)

I will have MANY MANY more opportunities in my next e-Book, so please be watching for that. Thank you for your interest!

XV. BEFORE YOU START

Before you launch off on your own as an entrepreneur, take some advice from someone who's "been there, done that." I thought having money at the onset wasn't important. I thought building hype about the business long before the opening wasn't important. I thought if you build it they would come! I think I even thought that, somehow, magically, it would all come together! Boy, was I wrong! So do the work and realize the importance of your business plan from the beginning, changing it as you go. To close this book, I decided to tell you a little more about my story and how I evolved into the "work-at-home entrepreneur" I am today. So here it is. I hope it helps you or gives you some ideas in how you can be successful.

MY STORY

In the beginning, I went in at 6:00 a.m. and stayed until 5:30pm. Yes, I was obsessed. And obsession is a major factor in success (see chapter 9), but you also have to have customers. And that's what I was lacking. It seems the strikes were against me in those early days of retail space business. I hired a sign guy to make my sign but on my opening day, he didn't show up! It also rained! The whole town practically shut down as we had intermittent downpours that day-my opening day! I was crushed! The only people that came to my opening day were my parents, and they brought me a coffee maker because the one I had leaked. I had hoped to serve coffee for my hundred or so passersby who I hoped would stop by that day! But no one came!

My parents were so nice and encouraging and we talked about the reasons I didn't have a successful opening day. The main reason was that I didn't get any customers! Or make any money! But looking back I realize that I hadn't had a succinct plan for getting and keeping customers. Perhaps my ad needed to be worked up better or I needed to advertise in more places. Perhaps I needed a PR manager to spread the word before I put out the OPEN sign for the first time. Perhaps I needed a sign! Perhaps…perhaps…perhaps.

Regardless of the reasons, I experienced only minimal success in those early days. I had prognosticated my figures way off too! I thought that I would have maybe 5 new clients a week. I was lucky if I got that many in a month. So I began to analyze my business plan, determine where it was lacking, and follow the money. And that's when I got smart. I believe that you can make anything work if you want it badly enough, but there has to be a **market** for it. And, I came to realize, through bitter tears, that my little town of 6500 was not my market. The whole world was my market. And that's when I realized instead of giving up, instead of minimizing, I needed to expand. And that's when I decided to move the business home and go "global."

Ironically, once I moved the business home, I started getting even more calls than ever before. I will never know whether this new interest in my business stemmed from the idea that people thought my business was no more, and people missed it, or the fact that once I moved home I got better at everything. It seems that for me, working in my home environment brings out the best in me, allows me to set my own goals and schedule and really focus on my business alone.

I have no children, and am single, so it helps that I only have a cockatiel to wake me up in the morning (which he does daily!) But my home has become my castle for creativity, my dome of knowledge, where I come up with and market new ideas. It is working for me. It can work for you in a similar fashion if you find something you are passionate about, something that makes money, and focus on your craft, and the market.

CONCLUSION

It is still a journey every single day for me. There are still days I wake up in a panic, like a captain of a ship that's gone into a storm. I feel as though I'm drowning at times, and looking for someone, anyone to save me! But then I realize that there's no one on the ship but me! I am truly on my own. And that's when I strap myself in, hang onto the helm and push onward! Because I am the captain of my own ship and whether I sink or swim, is all up to me!

I wish you all the best in your marvelous adventure as a work-at-home entrepreneur. If I can be of help to you in any way, or if you need me to write articles for your company to increase your traffic and conversions, or want to inquire about any of our other creative services, contact me at:
thestudiobydeb@suddenlink.net.

Thanks for buying my e-Book and happy sailing, captains!

CONTACT INFORMATION

http://smalltownglobal.com (Future corporate website—to launch in 2017)

Blog: http://smalltownglobal.blogspot.com "Media Creation in the Digital Age"

Face Book (add me!) http://www.facebook.com/DebKTechnerd

Twitter: http://www.twitter.com/thestudiobydeb

Email: thestudiobydeb1@gmail.com

Deborah Killion is a highly-paid online content writer, producer, and entrepreneur who works at home with her high tech multimedia production company and writing career. She has been featured by major publishers on You Tube as an expert at work-at-home opportunities. She plans to produce many more eBooks in the near future on this topic and others.

FOR FURTHER READING FROM MY ENTREPRENEUR MUSES:
(Note: *None of these people paid me to endorse their books. I did it on my own!*)

DAYMOND JOHN'S BOOK:
https://tb114.infusionsoft.com/app/storeFront/showProductDetail?productId=6

MARK CUBAN'S BOOK:
http://www.amazon.com/How-Win-Sport-Business-ebook/dp/B006AX6ONI/ref=sr_1_1?s=digital-text&ie=UTF8&qid=1380659043&sr=1-1&keywords=mark+cuban

KEVIN O'LEARY'S BOOK
http://www.amazon.com/Cold-Truth-Women-Money-ebook/dp/B00ADMR06C/ref=sr_1_1?s=digital-text&ie=UTF8&qid=1380659075&sr=1-1&keywords=kevin+o%27leary

BARBARA CORCORAN'S BOOK:
http://www.amazon.com/Shark-Tales-Turned-Billion-Business/dp/1591844185

Author's Note: I am a huge fan of ABC's "Shark Tank" and learn so much from what these guys say, as well as Lori and Robert. They have helped hundreds of budding entrepreneurs on their quest for success and they are my entrepreneur "muses." I have even chatted with them LIVE on Twitter during the broadcast of their weekly show on several different occasions. Check out their eBooks above after you've read mine and let them know what you think.

Also, be watching for my next ebook coming soon, entitled, "The Ultimate Guide to Legitimate Work-at-home Opportunities that Make REAL Money!" Coming soon!

To suggest specific topics you'd like to see me write about in the future that would help you on your quest for entrepreneurial freedom, email me at:
thestudiobydeb@suddenlink.net.

END

www.ingramcontent.com/pod-product-compliance
Lightning Source LLC
Chambersburg PA
CBHW070410190526
45169CB00003B/1198